First Phonics Words

Mairi Mackinnon

Illustrated by
Francesca Carabelli

cat

fat cat

cat on a mat

cat in a hat

How many cats with spots can you see?

a cat and a rat

Do you think the rat will get away?

bag

fun
bag

big bag

Can you say what all these bags are used for?

red bag

cat in
a bag

Do you have any bags like these?

Why do you think the dog at the top is sad?

Can you think of names for all the dogs?

Do you think the wet rat likes swimming?

Why is the little rat looking upset?

hat

top hat

sun hat

Can you see a warm hat to wear in winter?

big
hat

cat on
a hat

Which hats would be good for a party?

How many pigs can you see here?

pig in a pen

wet pig

Which pigs are running, standing, sitting?

What time of day is it in the picture?

Can you spot any eggs? How many?

bed

red bed

a man in bed

Who can you see sleeping in the beds?

bed on a rug

dog on a bed

Which bed would you like to have?

Oh no! What did the bad man do?

What sounds could you hear in this scene?

Why do you think the man is running?

Can you see any children on the big bus?

bug

bug on a bun

bug in a mug

What have all these bugs found to eat?

What would you like to eat at a picnic?

box

big box

hat box

Can you say what you'd put in each box?

Do you have any boxes like these at home?

van

red van

How many people are in the picture?

Why are they putting a bed in the van?

fox

bad fox

fox cub

Can you see any sleepy foxes?

What is the bad fox doing?

Guidance notes

About phonics

Phonics is a way of teaching children to read by breaking words down into combinations of sounds or **phonemes**. There are 44 phonemes in the English language. Some are represented by single letters, like the **c - a - t** sounds in the word **cat**. Others are represented by more than one letter, like the **sh - ar** sounds in the word **shark**.

Getting started

This book uses only the more basic phonemes, sounds made by a single letter, in short and easy-to-read words. It is a great way to encourage your child to take an interest in letters and words, and to build their confidence in the very early stages of reading.

Pronouncing phonemes

It's important to use the *sounds* of the letters, rather than the letter-names ("sss" not "ess"). You can find out how to say all the phonemes by listening to them on the Very First Reading website, **www.usborne.com/veryfirstreading*** – go to the **Resources** area and scroll down to **Pronouncing the phonemes**.

*US readers go to **www.veryfirstreading.com**

Sounding and blending

Show your child how to run the sounds together, or **blend** them, in order to read words. Read the phonemes separately at first, c - a - t, then read them more quickly, c-a-t, until you have run the sounds together to make **cat**. Encourage your child to try this too.

More words, more practice

Each double page has one simple word to read in large letters. Start by helping your child to read these words, and have fun spotting all the different bags or cats or foxes on the page and talking about them. When your child is more confident, try reading the smaller labels which introduce new words and short phrases.

Make reading fun

Reading is an important skill, but learning to read can be stressful for children *and* parents too. Help your child by making reading an enjoyable, shared activity. Look for fun details to talk about in the pictures. Read for just as long as your child wants to – short sessions can be very effective – and give plenty of praise and encouragement.

Edited by Jenny Tyler
Designed by Caroline Spatz
Digital manipulation by Nick Wakeford

First published in 2013 by Usborne Publishing Ltd., Usborne House,
83-85 Saffron Hill, London EC1N 8RT, England. www.usborne.com
Copyright © 2013 Usborne Publishing Ltd.

USBORNE VERY FIRST READING

There are over thirty titles in the **Usborne Very First Reading** series, which has been specially developed to help children learn to read. Here are some of them.

To find out more about the structure of the series, go to
www.usborne.com/veryfirstreading

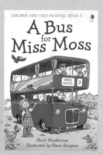

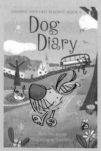